Washington Geography

Maps

Lessons

Vocabulary

Review Questions

Bonus Activities

WRITTEN BY
RANDY L. WOMACK, M.ED.
LEARNING DISABILITIES & BEHAVIOR DISORDERS

ILLUSTRATED BY
CHRISTINA "CHRIS" LEW

PUBLISHED BY

G.E.C. PUBLICATIONS

"LEADING THE WAY IN CREATIVE EDUCATIONAL MATERIALS" ™

857 LAKE BLVD. ❖ REDDING, CALIFORNIA 96003

This book is dedicated to my father, Jack Womack.
He's the greatest person I know. Thanks, Dad!

To Teachers and Parents

This book, *Washington Geography*, was written as a simplified, yet complete, resource book for you to use. The activities can be used as a supplemental resource for your regular geography curriculum.

There are seven separate sections in this book. The first two sections cover the basics in map reading and give the students a world overview. The other sections deal specifically with Washington's physical, economic, climatic and political features.

New vocabulary words are introduced at the beginning of each section. If your students are capable of looking up the words in a dictionary, please have them do so. You might even have them use the words in their own sentences. It is suggested that you, as the teacher, go over the words with your students *before* the lessons are actually begun, making sure that the meanings are understood by the children. This will help your students grasp the concepts being taught.

The lessons are reinforced with maps, exercises, review questions and bonus activities. The review questions can be used as tests, but we deliberately omitted the word "test" because many children fall apart at the notion of one. An optional (☆☆) Bonus Activity is at the end of each section. As the teacher, you should be the one to choose which students are capable of completing the research involved. (Please feel free to add your own ideas to expand on these activities.)

We hope you and your students enjoy this book — as well as learn a lot about the state of Washington.

Randy L. Womack
Author

Copyright ©1996, 1990 **GOLDEN EDUCATIONAL CENTER**
ALL RIGHTS RESERVED – PRINTED IN U.S.A.
PUBLISHED BY GOLDEN EDUCATIONAL CENTER
857 LAKE BLVD.❖ REDDING, CALIFORNIA 96003

™

ISBN 1–56500–036-6

Washington Geography
Section Contents

Vocabulary Words ❖ Maps ❖ Questions
☆☆ Bonus Activities
Included in the First Seven Sections of This Book

Washington
The Evergreen State

Washington
Geography
World Overview

New Words to Learn:

Find the words in a dictionary and write the meanings on the line.

1. **cartographer:** _____

2. **climate:** _____

3. **compass:** _____

4. **continent:** _____

5. **geographer:** _____

6. **globe:** _____

7. **international date line:** _____

8. **orient(ed):** _____

9. **observatory:** _____

10. **scientist:** _____

11. **sphere:** _____

Washington
World Overview

Name _____

Date _____

What is Geography?

Many **scientists** are **geographers**. They study the planet earth and different types of life on it.

There are many different types of geographers. Some study about the animals, others study about the **climate**, or about the people and where they live. They also study about plant life, the surface of the earth and how the earth changes. Some of them even study about the oceans.

Geographers who study all of the different things just mentioned often combine the information they have learned.

Cartographers work closely with geographers. A cartographer is a person who makes maps. Maps can be made of very large areas such as the stars in space. They can be made of the entire earth, only one **continent** or ocean floor or perhaps only one country or state. You could even make a map that just shows the rooms in your house, apartment or school. Maps are important to us so we can have knowledge about any area of interest.

Making maps of the world is not easy. Cartographers must be very accurate. It is very difficult to be accurate on maps of the entire earth. You see, the earth is a **sphere**. Maps are usually drawn on flat paper. However, **globes** are quite accurate because they are maps placed on a sphere.

In schools all over the world, students are taught many things about the geography of the earth. They learn about direction, climate, the earth's surface and how to read maps. With the help of maps, they learn about the people, plants and animals of earth. They also study about the part of the world in which they live.

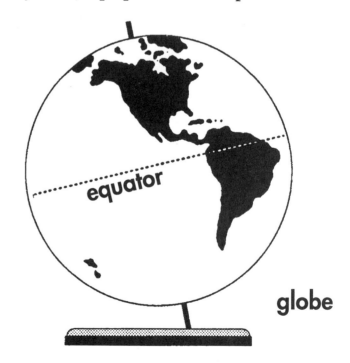

globe

Washington
World Overview

Which Way Is Up?

Before you learn specific things about the state of Washington, it is important that you know certain things about the entire world, including the oceans and continents.

When reading a map of the world, you must always keep in mind that you are looking down on the map, as if you were in an airplane. Also you must think about the directions of north, east, west and south. Cartographers print **compass** roses on maps to show the direction the map is **oriented**.

North is at the top. South is at the bottom — the opposite of north.

East is to the right. West is to the left — the opposite of east.

Do these things using the map below.

1. Use a ruler and divide the circle into halves by connecting the two dots.

2. On the lines below, spell the correct direction around the circle. (It would be a *sphere* if you could hold it.) Color the north half of the circle yellow or orange. Color the south half of the circle blue or purple.

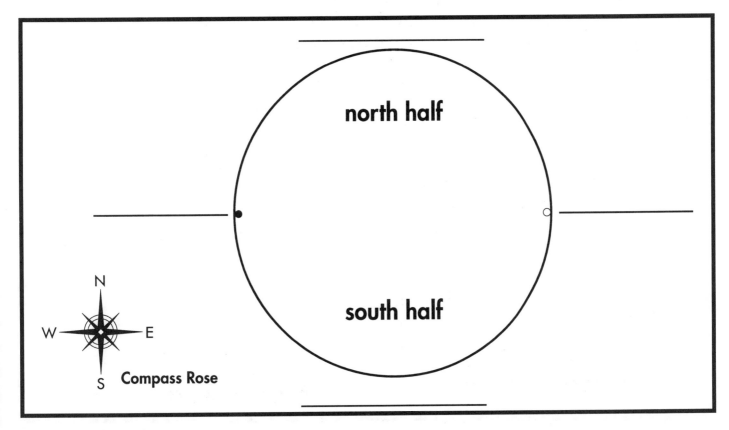

Name _____

Date _____

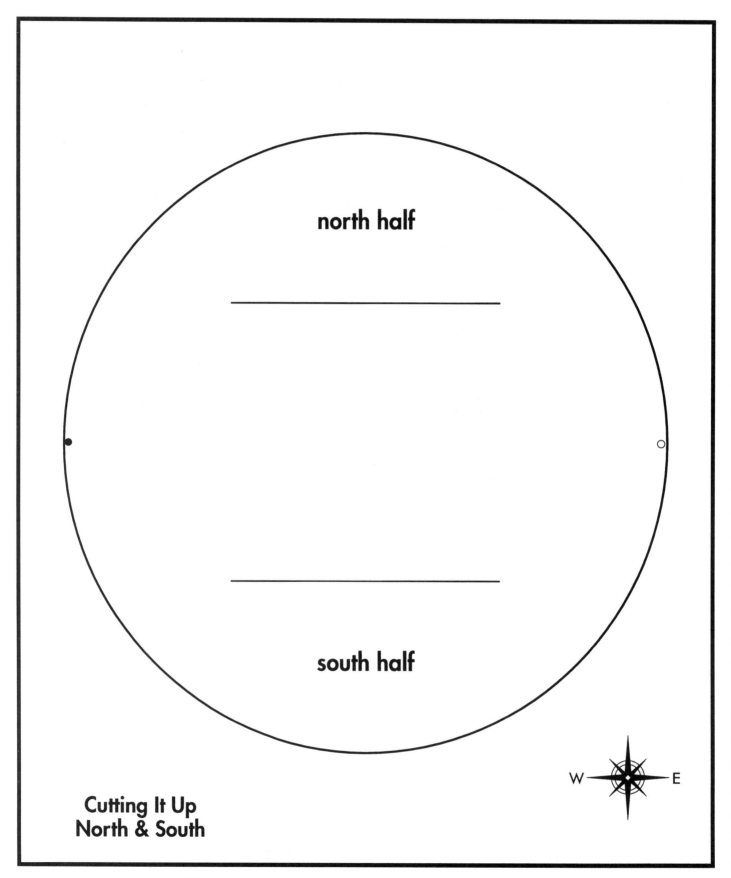

north half

_____

_____

south half

Cutting It Up
North & South

W ✦ E

Name _____

Date _____

Cutting It Up — North & South

Remember that the earth is actually a sphere or shaped like a ball, not a flat circle. When you are looking at one side of the earth you cannot see the other side. That is why when it is daytime where you live, it is nighttime for the people on the other side of the world.

> You can get a flashlight and a ball and see for yourself. Put a small piece of tape on the ball and shine the flashlight onto it. As the light hits the tape on the ball, slowly turn the ball. Notice the position of your tape and the shadow and the light.

Notice the two half-circles and the directions on page 5. If you cut the earth in half like this, you would have a northern half and a southern half. Geographers do this exact thing in order to be more specific about directions and where things are on earth.

They use a long word to describe the two halves — **hemisphere**. However, it is not hard to understand. *Hemi* means half. *Sphere* — as you already know — means shaped like a ball. Put them together and you get, half of a sphere (or ball).

Do these things using the map provided.

1. Use a ruler and divide the circle into semi-circles by connecting the two dots with a straight line.

Now look at the two half-circles (hemispheres) on page 6. On the lines provided, do the following things:

2. Write *Northern Hemisphere* in the north half of the circle.

3. Write *Southern Hemisphere* in the south half of the circle.

4. Now that you know where the northern & southern hemispheres are, write your first name inside the northern hemisphere. Write your last name inside the southern hemisphere.

5. Write your middle name right on top of the line that divides the northern and southern hemispheres.

6. Complete the compass rose by writing *N* for north and *S* for south. You can color your completed map if you like.

Washington
World Overview

Name _____

Date _____

W   E

Equal Halves
North & South

Name _____

Date _____

Equal Halves — North & South

Look at the last lesson where you wrote your names inside the different hemispheres. You should have written your middle name exactly on top of the line in the middle. This line separates the northern and southern halves, making them two **equal** parts.

Cartographers (map makers) use an imaginary line in the middle of the earth that runs from the left (west) to the right (east). It is exactly like the one you wrote your middle name on. It is in the exact middle of the earth. It separates the northern hemisphere from the southern hemisphere. Cartographers and geographers have given this imaginary line a name just like you did. They have named it the *equator*.

Notice that the word *equal* and the word *equator* are very similar in spelling and sound. They also mean about the same thing.

Equal means that at least two things are the same.
  (1+2 means the same thing as 3.)

The equator is the imaginary line that divides the earth into the two equal parts of north and south. In order for the equator to divide the earth equally, it must be exactly in the middle and go completely around the earth. The continents located mostly above the equator are in the northern hemisphere. The continents mostly located south of the equator are in the southern hemisphere. (How appropriate!)

Do these things using the map provided.

1. Use a ruler to draw an equator on the two shapes. Connect the west dot (solid black) and east dot (outlined) on each of the circles.

2. Label the blank circle and the one with the map exactly the same. Use all of the words below to label them.

    North   **South**   **East**   **West**   **Northern Hemisphere**

              Equator   **Southern Hemisphere**

3. Complete the compass rose by writing *N* for north and *S* for south.

4. Color the hemispheres and the two continents as nicely as you can.

Name _____

Date _____

_____

_____   _____

_____

Cutting It Up
East & West

Cutting It Up — East & West

Cartographers also use an imaginary line in the middle of the earth that runs from the top (north) to the bottom (south). It is in the exact middle of the earth, also. It separates the eastern hemisphere from the western hemisphere. Cartographers and geographers have given this imaginary line a name just like they did for the equator. They have named it the *prime meridian.*

These words are also easy to understand. Look at the meanings of the words and they will make sense to you.

Prime means the beginning, or the original of something.

Meridian means the "middle of the day". When the sun is directly over a meridian line, it is noon there — the middle of the day.

Use a ruler to connect the north dot (solid black) and south dot (outlined) shown on the circle. This first meridian line is the prime meridian. The western and eastern halves of the earth meet at this line.

As you follow the prime meridian, at 0° (zero degrees), around to the other side of the earth, it changes into the **international date line**, at 180° (one hundred eighty degrees). When it is noon at the prime meridian, it is midnight at the international date line. (Remember, at midnight, night turns into morning, even if it is dark.)

Do these things using the map provided.

1. Label the prime meridian you drew when you connected the two dots.

2. Complete the compass rose by writing *N* for north, *S* for south, *E* for east and *W* for west.

3. Write North, East, West and South on the correct lines.

4. Color the west half of the map a light color.

5. Color the east half of the map a darker color than the west half.

> You can test this information for yourself by using some tape and a ball like you did on page seven. This time run tape around the middle of the ball running north and south. Label one side the prime meridian and the other the international date line. Use a flashlight to experiment the different times of day by turning the ball and holding the light still.

Washington
World Overview

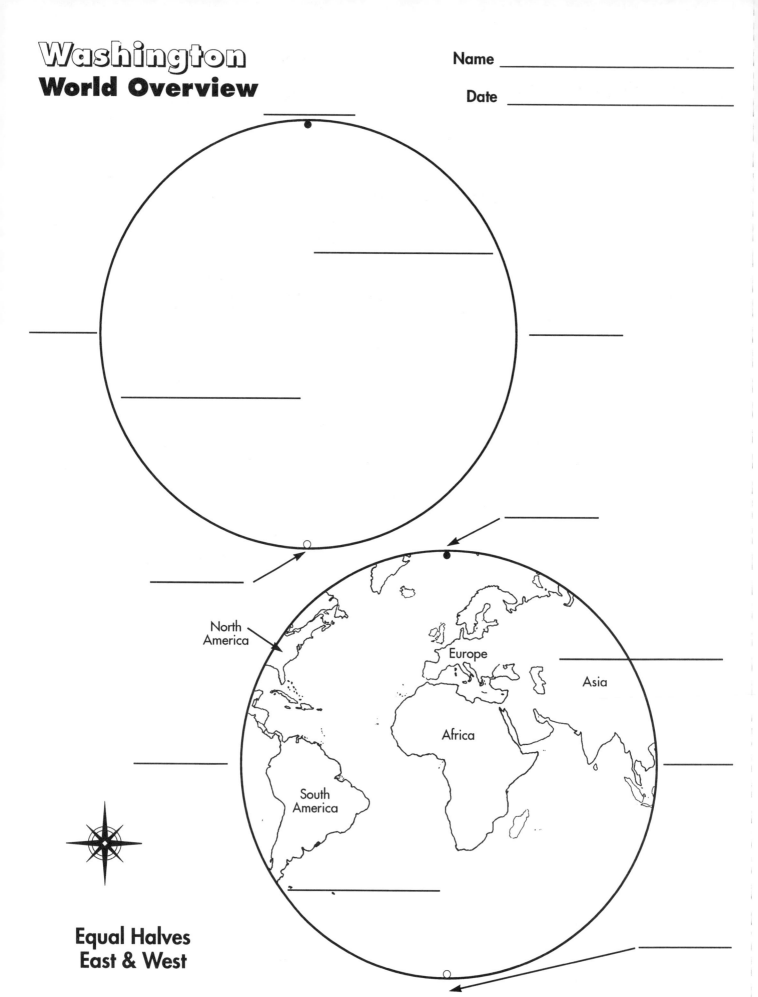

Equal Halves
East & West

North
America

Europe

Asia

Africa

South
America

Equal Halves — East & West

The meridian lines of the earth are important for cartographers to measure east and west distances on the earth. Geographers had to determine where the first meridian would be located so everyone would start counting from the same place. They called this the prime meridian.

In 1884, geographers met in Washington, D.C. to discuss where the prime meridian would be located. They decided that it would pass through the **observatory** at Greenwich, England. This imaginary line officially divided the earth into eastern and western halves.

Just like the equator divides the earth into northern and southern hemispheres, the prime meridian divides the earth into eastern and western hemispheres. The continents located mostly east of the prime meridian are in the eastern hemisphere. The continents located mostly west of the prime meridian are in the western hemisphere. (That makes sense!)

Do these things using the map provided.

1. Use a ruler to draw a prime meridian on the two shapes. Connect the north (solid black) and south (outlined) dots on each of the circles.

2. Complete the compass rose by writing *N* for north, *S* for south, *E* for east and *W* for west.

3. Label the blank circle and the one with the map exactly the same. Use all of the words below to label them.

North   South   East   West   Eastern Hemisphere

Prime Meridian   Western Hemisphere

4. Which continents are located in the western hemisphere?

_____   _____

5. Color the hemispheres and continents as nicely as you can.

Look at the map provided. Notice that the prime meridian passes through the continents of Europe and Africa. Geographers decided that these two continents would be considered part of the eastern hemisphere. They made this decision because most of the continents' land is already in the eastern hemisphere.

Washington
World Overview

Name _____

Date _____

REVIEW QUESTIONS

Circle the best answer to each question.

1. What does geography mean?
   a. making maps   b. study of the earth   c. science

2. What geometric shape is the earth?
   a. hemisphere   b. circle   c. sphere   d. flat

3. What is the most accurate type of map?
   a. globe   b. paper   c. flat   d. street

Write the correct answer to complete the sentences.

4. The bottom half of the earth is called the _____ .

5. The equator is an _____ line to divide the _____ in half.

6. _____ make maps.

7. The _____ is the imaginary line that divides the
   _____ into the eastern and the _____ hemispheres.

Write the correct (best) answer on the line from the list of bold words.

a. prime _____   **right**

b. north _____   **"middle of the day"**

c. hemi _____   **half**

d. south _____   **beginning**

e. east _____   **middle line**

f. west _____   **bottom**

g. sphere _____   **top**

h. equator _____   **ball-shaped**

i. meridian _____   **left**

List 6 things geographers study. _____ _____

_____ _____ _____ _____

☆☆ **Bonus Activity**
Using another resource book, write a report about one of earth's continents, oceans, a
famous scientist or an animal. Find or make pictures to go with your report.

Washington Geography: **World Overview**   14   © GOLDEN EDUCATIONAL CENTER

New Words to Learn:
Find the words in a dictionary and write the meanings on the line.

1. **coast:** _____

2. **country:** _____

3. **degree:** _____

4. **independent:** _____

5. **lateral** (latitude): _____

6. **longitude:** _____

7. **peninsula:** _____

Washington
Locating Washington

Name _____

Date _____

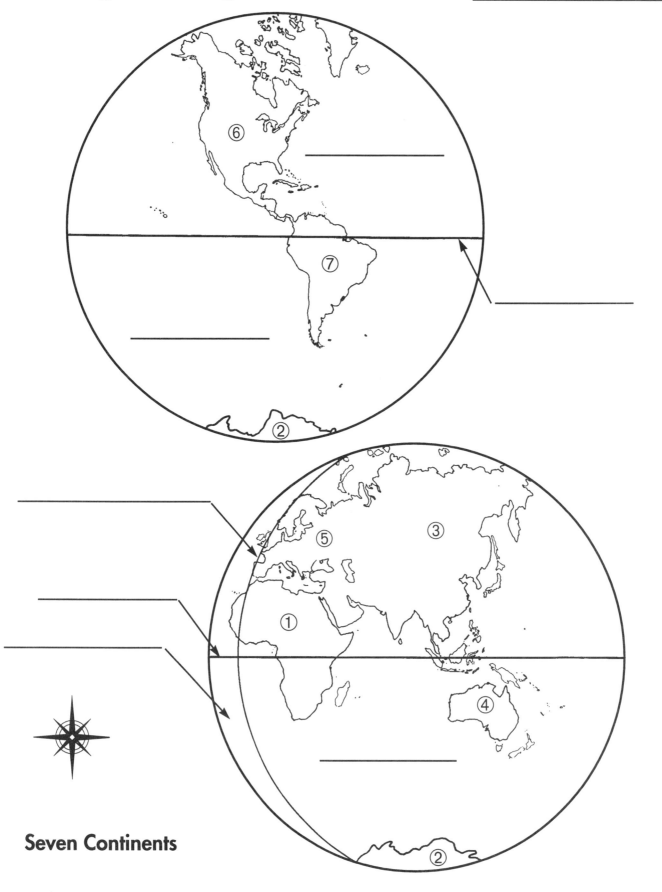

Seven Continents

Seven Continents

One of the meanings of the word *continent* is *self-contained*. There are seven land forms in the world that are called continents. They are nearly all surrounded by water, which makes them self-contained. They are also very large areas of land. Geographers also consider the nearby islands part of the continent they are closest to.

The seven continents of the world are **Asia, Africa, Antarctica, Australia, Europe, North America,** and **South America**. (Technically, however, Europe is not a continent, but a **peninsula** of Asia. It is part of what could be called *the Eurasian continent*.)

The imaginary boundary line separating Europe and Asia was determined by geographers many years ago. They made the boundary where it is because there are mountain ranges (the Ural and Caucasus Mountains) that act as natural barriers. Mountains were very difficult to get across many years ago without modern planes, trains or cars.

Eastern & Western Continents

Geographers often talk about the continents of the eastern hemisphere and the western hemisphere. In order to make maps showing the two hemispheres of the earth, cartographers often make the continents in their own circle, just like the maps you see.

North America and South America are the two continents in the western hemisphere. The continents in the eastern hemisphere are Africa, Asia, Europe and Australia. Antarctica is in the southern hemisphere.

Do these things using the map provided.

Write the correct names of the continents by the correct number. Write the other words in the correct places. Color your maps.

Africa ①   Antarctica ②   Asia ③   Australia ④   Europe ⑤

North America ⑥   South America ⑦   North   East   West   South

Southern Hemisphere   Eastern Hemisphere   Western Hemisphere

Equator   Northern Hemisphere   Prime Meridian

Complete the compass rose.

Washington
Locating Washington

Name _____

Date _____

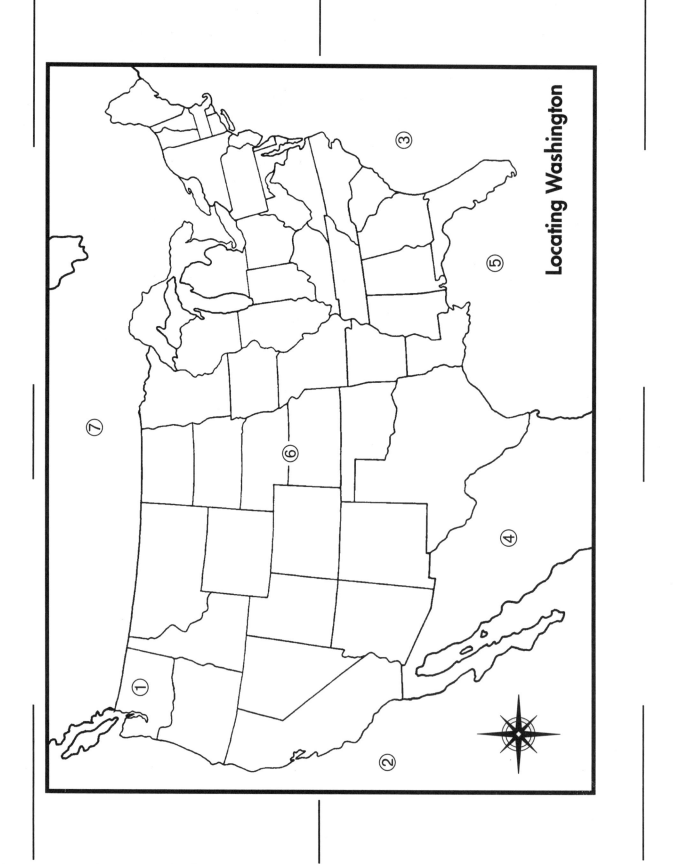

Locating Washington

North & South America

When the continents of North America and South America were first discovered, they were just called *America* or the *New World* by Europeans. Eventually, the continent south of the equator was named South America. The continent north of the equator came to be called North America. (Once again, very appropriate.) Within each of these continents, there are several independent countries. Our **country**, the United States, is located within North America.

Washington State

There are fifty individual states within the United States. Washington is one of the states in the United States. It was the 42nd state admitted to the Union.

Washington is the most northern state on the west **coast**. Washington is in the *northwest* corner of the United States (Alaska not included). To determine northwest, you must move north at the same time you move west. To go southeast, you must move south at the same time you move east.

Do these things using the map provided.

1. Write these directional words in the correct location. Write them on the lines outside of the frame.

   North   **East**   **West**   **South**

   Southeast   **Northwest**   **Southwest**   **Northeast**

2. Write the correct names of the places by the correct number. Use all the words provided.

   Washington ①   **Pacific Ocean** ②   **Atlantic Ocean** ③

   Mexico ④   **Gulf of Mexico** ⑤   **United States** ⑥   **Canada** ⑦

3. Color Washington on the map a bright color like yellow, orange or red.

4. Make the rest of the United States and Canada any other color but blue.

5. Complete the compass rose by writing *N, E, W* and *S* in the correct places.

6. Color the water on the map blue.

Name _____

Date _____

Back to the Equator & Prime Meridian

Remember that the equator and the prime meridian are the imaginary lines that divide the earth in the middle. The equator divides the north from the south, while the prime meridian divides the east from the west.

If you look at a globe or some maps, you will notice that there are other lines much like the equator and prime meridian lines. Some run north and south and meet at the poles. These are called **meridians**, with the first one being the prime meridian. (Remember: *prime* means *beginning*.) The meridian lines are also called **longitude** lines.

You can remember which way the *longitude* and *latitude* lines "run" by remembering the following things:

1. Longitude has the word "long" in it.
   The *long lines* always go from top-to-bottom.

2. Now stand up and walk sideways exactly like this:
   (a.) Keep facing forward.
   (b.) Step with your right foot to your right side.
   (c.) Slide your left foot to meet your right foot
   Your ankles should almost touch each other.
   (d.) Do this to the right for a few steps, then do the
   opposite to the left. You were moving *laterally*.

   Latitude lines run just the way you moved, from side-to-side.

The lines that are north and south of the equator are called latitude lines. These latitude lines run all the way around the earth. They stay the same distance from the equator all the way around it. As they get closer to the north and south poles, the lines are not as long as the equator because the earth is smaller near the top and bottom.

You can see this for yourself. Get a medium or large ball and some tape. Put tape around the ball where the equator would be. Then put some around the ball near the top or bottom of it. Remove both pieces of tape and see which one is longer.

Washington
Locating Washington

Name _____

Date _____

Remember that latitude and longitude (meridian) lines are only imaginary. They are needed by geographers, sailors and others in order to locate places on the earth.

Geographers have given each of the imaginary lines (latitude lines and longitude lines) a number in **degrees**. The equator and prime meridian are numbered zero degrees (0°). The degrees measure the distance from one line to the next. They are always the same distance apart. There are 180° east *and* 180° west that measure half way around the earth from the prime meridian. These imaginary lines meet on the other side of the earth, directly opposite of the prime meridian. Where they meet is the international date line. (Remember, this is where midnight turns into the next morning when it is noon at the prime meridian.) The latitude lines run from the equator to 90° north and 90° south.

Plot numbers on the map below.

1. Follow the two lines until they meet and draw a dot.
   Write the correct number by the dot you drew.

   6W & 3N ①   **9E & 2N** ②   **8W & 4S** ③   **0 & 4N** ④   **8E & 3S** ⑤

2. Use a ruler and connect the dots in numerical order (1 to 2, 2 to 3, etc.).
   Connect number 5 to number 1.

3. Color the picture you made on your map.

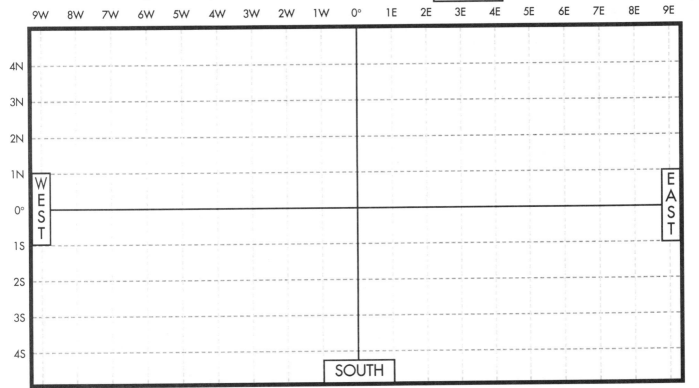

Name _____

Date _____

The letters **N**, **E**, **W** and **S** are always written after the number and degrees sign. These letters stand for north, east, west and south. You must use the directional letter or you will not know exactly where the location is. See these examples:

30°W means 30° west of the prime meridian.

60°E means 60° east of the prime meridian.

15°S means 15° south of the equator.

45°N means 45° north of the equator.

Do these things using the map below.

1. Label the prime meridian (PM) and equator (Eq).
2. From the prime meridian, draw a ★ at 30°E & 45°N from the equator.
3. From the equator, draw a ♣ at 15°S & 105°E from the prime meridian.
4. From the equator draw a ♥ at 30°N & 75°W from the prime meridian.
5. From the prime meridian, draw a ➤ at 90°W & 60°S from the equator.

Note: Remember that the first section of this book explained that it is difficult to make accurate flat maps. This is a great example. The equator and prime meridian pass through the continents where they should. However, the longitude and latitude lines are not equally spaced as they should be. Now you see one problem cartographers have.

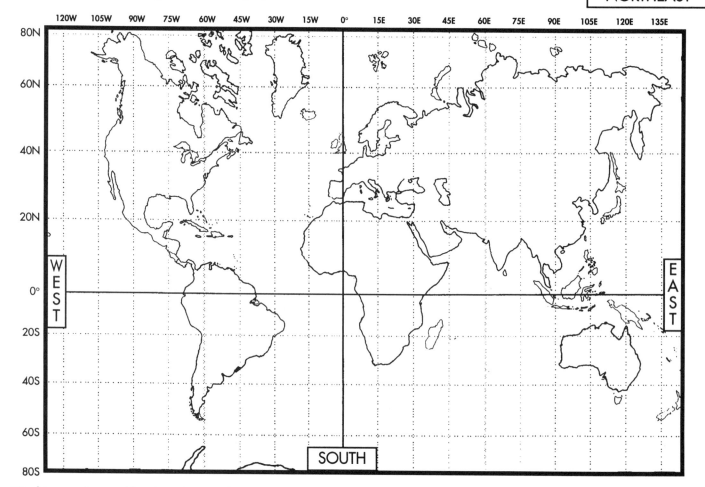

Washington
Locating Washington

Name _____

Date _____

REVIEW QUESTIONS

(Page 1 of 2)

Write the correct answer in the space provided.

Write the names of the seven continents in alphabetical order.
Make sure you capitalize the names.

1. _____   4. _____

2. _____   5. _____

3. _____   6. _____

7. _____

Write the names of the continents in the western hemisphere.
Write them in alphabetical order. Not all of the lines will be used.

1. _____   4. _____

2. _____   5. _____

3. _____   6. _____

7. _____

Write the names of the continents mostly in the eastern hemisphere.
Write them in alphabetical order. Not all of the lines will be used.

1. _____   4. _____

2. _____   5. _____

3. _____   6. _____

7. _____

Write the names of the continents mostly in the southern hemisphere.
Write them in alphabetical order. Not all of the lines will be used.

1. _____   4. _____

2. _____   5. _____

3. _____   6. _____

7. _____

Washington
Locating Washington

Name _____

Date _____

REVIEW QUESTIONS

(Page 2 of 2)

Write the correct answer in the space provided. (You may need to use a map.)

1. Which directions do longitude lines run? _____

2. Explain what lateral means. _____

3. Which latitude line is at zero degrees (0°)? _____

4. Which longitude line is at zero degrees (0°)? _____

5. Name the ocean off the west coast of Washington. _____

6. What country is north of Washington? _____

7. What country is south of the United States? _____

8. From Washington, what direction is the east coast of the U.S.? _____

9. In which corner of the United States is Washington located? _____

10. From California, what direction is Washington? _____

11. From the Atlantic Ocean, what direction is Washington? _____

12. From Florida, what direction is Washington? _____

13. From Canada's east coast, what direction is Washington? _____

14. About how many longitude degrees wide is Washington? _____

15. About how many latitude degrees high is Washington? _____

16. From the southern tip of Mexico, near the Gulf of Mexico, what direction is Washington? _____

17. Which 2 hemispheres have the most land? _____

☆☆ Bonus Activity
Using another resource book, write a report about a country or continent that the prime meridian or equator pass through. Make maps and pictures to go along with your report. Write about the climate, people, land regions or other interesting things.

New Words to Learn:

Find the words in a dictionary and write the meanings on the line.

1. **canyon:** _____

2. **crust:** _____

3. **economic:** _____

4. **erupt:** _____

5. **fertile:** _____

6. **industry:** _____

7. **plateau:** _____

8. **range:** _____

9. **topographical:** _____

10. **volcano:** _____

11. **valley:** _____

Washington
Physical Features

Name _____

Date _____

Six Main Land Regions

1. *Olympic Mountains*   2. *Coast Range*   3. *Puget Sound Lowland*

4. *Cascade Mountains*   5. *Columbia Plateau*   6. *Rocky Mountains*

The *Olympic Mountains*, in the northwest corner of Washington, are bordered on the north by the Strait of Juan de Fuca (WAN dey FOOkuh) and the Pacific Ocean on the west. Most of the region is part of the Olympic National Park. The Olympic Mountains form one of the wildest areas in the entire United States. It is a very rugged, snow-capped mountain **range**, with the highest peak being Mount Olympus. This mountain peak rises to 7,965 (2,428 m) feet above sea level. The mountains are so rugged that many areas have never been explored. Logging in the foothills of the mountains is this region's main industry.

The *Coast Range* covers the southwest corner of the state and extends southward into the state of Oregon. The *Willapa Hills* are the main land feature of the region. The elevation of these hills is not at all close to the Olympic Mountains. *Walville Peak* is the highest peak in this region. However, it is only 2,420 feet (738 m) above sea level. Logging and lumber milling are the region's most important **economic** activities. In addition to logging, many people work in the fishing **industry** and dairy industry.

The *Puget* (PUE-jet) *Sound Lowland* is a plain that is in between the Olympic Mountains and Coast Range on the west and the Cascade Mountains on the east. This region extends northward to British Columbia, Canada, and southward to Oregon. The Chehalis River Valley is also part of this region. This **valley** extends westward to the Pacific Ocean. Puget Sound is a huge bay that is almost completely surrounded by land. The Strait of Juan de Fuca connects Puget Sound to the Pacific Ocean.

About three-fourths of the state's people live in this lowland region. The region also has about three-fifths of the state's cities and most of its factories and sawmills.

Note: *The Strait of Juan de Fuca was named after the 1592 Spanish explorer Juan de Fuca. Puget Sound was named after Peter Puget, the lieutenant of the English explorer, Captain George Vancouver.*

Washington
Physical Features

Land Regions

The *Cascade Mountains*, located east of the Puget Sound Lowland, separate the western part of the state from the eastern part. The Cascade Mountains of Washington are part of a long mountain range that stretches from Canada to northern California. The peaks of several volcanoes rise high above the main chain of mountains. Most of the **volcanoes** are supposed to be inactive. However, on May 18, 1980, Mount Saint Helens **erupted**. Before this volcano erupted its elevation was 9,677 feet (2,950 m) above sea level. Today it is several hundred feet lower. Mount Rainier, another volcano, is the highest point in Washington, and one of the highest peaks in the entire United States. It is 14,410 feet (4,392 m) above sea level. Other high peaks in Washington's Cascade Mountain Range include Mount Adams (12,307 feet or 3,751 m); Mount Baker (10,778 feet or 3,285 m); and Glacier Peak (10,541 feet or 3,213 m). All of these mountains have permanent snow-capped tops and large forests on their lower slopes.

The *Columbia **Plateau*** covers most of the central and southeastern portion of Washington. This basin is surrounded by higher land in Washington, Idaho and Oregon. This area makes up one of the largest lava plateaus in the entire world. It is believed by many scientists that the basin was formed by lava which flowed from cracks in the earth's **crust** hundreds of years ago.

There are many interesting **canyons** in the Columbia Plateau. Parts of this region have very **fertile** land. Other parts of the desert-like Columbia Basin are good for growing crops when the land is irrigated. The Palouse country in the southeast has deep, fertile soil that makes up gentle rolling hills. This soil holds in moisture and allows dry farming. In this area Washington's most important crop, wheat, is grown.

The *Rocky Mountains* cut across the northeastern corner of the state. This *branch* of the Rocky Mountains is sometimes called the Columbia Mountains. These mountains are rich with several minerals, including clay, copper, gold, lead, limestone, magnesium, silver, and zinc. The Rockies are the highest and longest range in North America. It starts in northern Alaska and continues south into northern New Mexico (over 3,000 miles). The Rockies form the Continental Divide, which separates rivers that flow west to the Pacific Ocean from those flowing southeast to the Gulf of Mexico, and eventually to the Atlantic Ocean.

Washington
Physical Features

Name _____

Date _____

Complete this map.

1. Complete the compass rose.

2. Label each of the land regions by writing the name by the correct number.

3. Color the land region where you live your favorite color.

4. Color each of the other regions a different color.

Washington's six main land regions:

Olympic Mountains ①   **Coast Range** ②   **Puget Sound Lowland** ③

Cascade Mountains ④   **Columbia Plateau** ⑤   **Rocky Mountains** ⑥

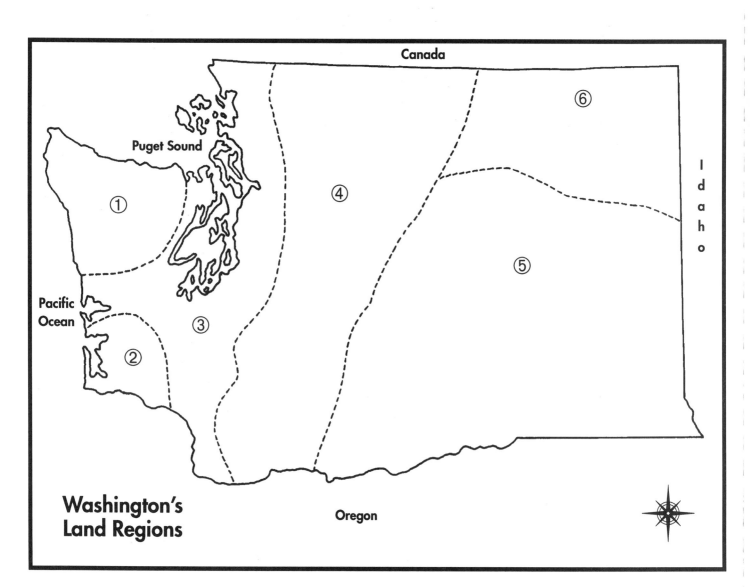

Washington's Land Regions

Washington
Physical Features

Topographical maps are maps that show the features of the land's surface. They show the mountains, rivers and lakes. They also show man-made features like roads, bridges and canals. You can make a topographical map of Washington by following the directions on this page.

Complete this map... (Complete the compass rose first.)

1. Trace over the (– – – – – – – –) lines with black ink or pencil to make the interstate expressways.

2. Trace over the (• • • • • • • • • • • • •) lines with blue ink or pencil to make the major rivers.

3. Draw each of the symbols below to show Washington's topography.

mountains ①   **forests ②**   **shrubs & grass ③**   **farmland ④**

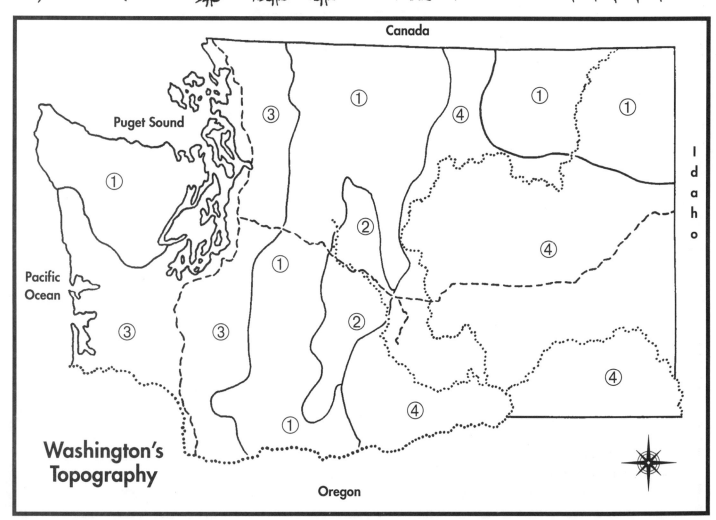

Washington's Topography

Washington
Physical Features

Name _____

Date _____

Explain where each of the land regions is and tell something about it.

1. *Olympic Mountains* _____

_____

_____

❖ ❖ ❖ ❖ ❖

2. *Coast Range* _____

_____

_____

❖ ❖ ❖ ❖ ❖

3. *Puget Sound Lowland* _____

_____

_____

❖ ❖ ❖ ❖ ❖

4. *Cascade Mountains* _____

_____

_____

❖ ❖ ❖ ❖ ❖

5. *Rocky Mountains* _____

_____

_____

❖ ❖ ❖ ❖ ❖

6. *Columbia Plateau* _____

_____

_____

❖ ❖ ❖ ❖ ❖

7. Explain what a topographical map shows _____

_____

☆☆ **Bonus Activity**
Using another resource book, write a report about one of Washington's land regions,
bordering country or state, the Continental Divide or a national park or state park located
in Washington. Make or find pictures to go along with your report.

Washington Geography
Economic Features

New Words to Learn:

Find the words in a dictionary and write the meanings on the line.

1. **acre:**_____

2. **agriculture:**_____

3. **average:** _____

4. **bulb** (flower):_____

5. **conserve:**_____

6. **deposit** (mineral):_____

7. **economy:**_____

8. **generate:** _____

9. **hops** (noun): _____

10. **irrigate:**_____

11. **mineral:** _____

Washington
Economic Features

Name _____

Date _____

Complete this map... (Complete the compass rose first.)

Draw the symbols by the correct number.

fruit ① 🍎

dairy products ②

potatoes ③

berries ④

sheep/wool products ⑤

wheat/grain ⑥

vegetables ⑦ (choose one)

grapes ⑧

poultry ⑨

fish ⑩

shellfish ⑪ (choose one)

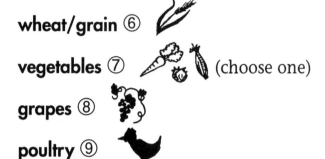

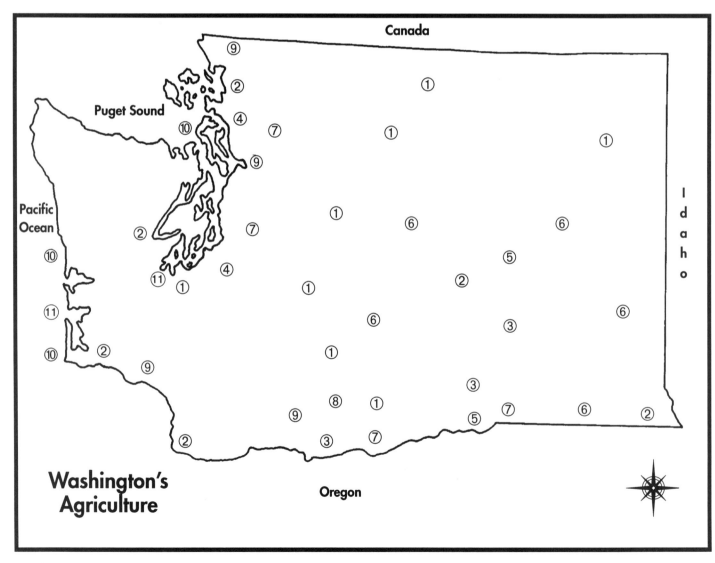

Washington's Agriculture

Canada

Puget Sound

Pacific Ocean

Idaho

Oregon

Name _____

Date _____

Agriculture

Washington has about 33,500 farms. These **average** about 450 **acres** in size. **Agriculture** accounts for about 19% of Washington's total **economy**.

Farmers produce crops by dry farming methods and by **irrigation**. Farmers in the eastern part of the state grow spring and winter wheat. The main farming areas with irrigation are in the Columbia Basin and in the valleys of the Okanogan, Snake, Spokane, Walla Walla, Wenatchee, and Yakima rivers.

Wheat is Washington's most valuable crop. Washington is the leading state in the production of dry peas. It is also first in the production of **hops**, which are used in the making of beer. Washington also ranks high in the production of potatoes, grown mainly in the south-central part of the state. The state is also among the leading producers of dry beans, barley, asparagus, green peas and other grains.

Washington state grows more apples than any other state in the United States. Red and Golden Delicious are two of the kinds of apples that are enjoyed throughout the nation. Washington also ranks high in the production of apricots, cherries, pears, plums and prunes. Washington also produces a lot of raspberries, blueberries, strawberries, and cranberries. It also ranks high in grape production.

In addition to the above farming products, Washington is one of the world's largest producers of iris and daffodil **bulbs**. The Puyallup, Skagit and the lower Cowlitz river valleys are world-famous for growing these and other flower bulbs.

Color the daffodil, the iris and "Dandy Lion."

These are definitely not to scale!

Washington
Economic Features

Complete this map...

1. Draw logs (or write the word) by the correct number.

   forest products ①

2. Write the name of the ore under the correct number.

   coal ②   **silver** ④   **zinc** ⑥

   gold ③   **lead** ⑤   **copper** ⑦

   magnesium ⑧

3. Complete the compass rose.

> Compare the Washington Land Region map in section three to the one below. Notice that the minerals in this map are all located in mountain ranges. They are not in any of the lowland or plateau regions.

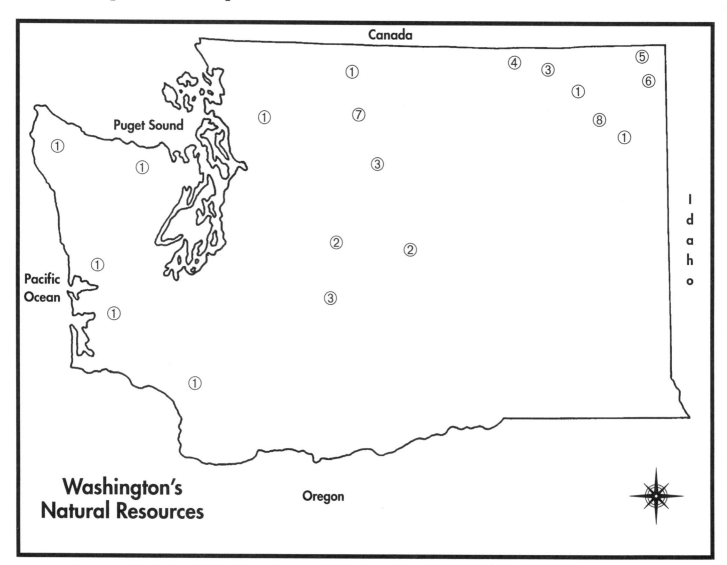

Washington's Natural Resources

Washington
Economic Features

Name _____

Date _____

Natural Resources

Washington has many natural resources. The state has a plentiful supply of water, large timber forests, and rich, fertile soil.

Water is one of the state's most important resources. The melted snow from the mountain regions flows to the rivers and provides the water that industry needs to operate. The water is also used for **generating** electrical power, irrigation and home use. The inlets and bays of Puget Sound and along the coast help the shipping and commercial fishing industries to prosper. The abundance of water also helps the pleasure boating industry.

Forests cover about 23 million acres in the state. Almost 18 million of the acres can be used for the timber industry. The leading timber tree west of the Cascade Mountain Range is the western hemlock. Douglas fir, Sitka spruce and the western red cedar are also very common in the western part of the state. The Douglas fir tree is the main timber tree in the drier eastern section of the state.

The state government, the U.S. government and many private companies work very hard to **conserve** Washington's timber resources. They are always planting small trees or scattering seeds from helicopters to help replenish the trees that have been cut for timber.

The only large coal **deposits** on the Pacific Coast are located in Washington. The largest coal deposits are found in western Washington, especially Lewis County. Gold is mined on the eastern slopes of the Cascade Mountains and the Okanogan Mountains.

The Washington salmon have an interesting life story. They are also a very popular fish to catch as a sport because they are great fighters. The salmon are also very important to commercial fishermen because of the high price they bring.

Washington
Economic Features

Name _____

Date _____

REVIEW QUESTIONS

Write the correct answer in the space provided.

1. What is Washington's most important crop? _____

2. Write the names of the vegetables and grains produced in Washington. Write them in alphabetical order.

   1. _____   5. _____

   2. _____   6. _____

   3. _____   7. _____

   4. _____   8. _____

3. Write the names of the fruits and berries produced in Washington. Write them in alphabetical order.

   1. _____   7. _____

   2. _____   8. _____

   3. _____   9. _____

   4. _____   10. _____

   5. _____   11. _____

   6. _____

4. Name the three natural resources that are the most plentiful in Washington.

   1. _____   2. _____   3. _____

5. Explain how Washington's timber resources are replenished.

   _____

   _____

6. Where are the largest coal deposits in Washington? _____

7. Explain why water is one of Washington's most important natural resources.

   _____

   _____

☆☆ **Bonus Activity**
Using another resource book, write a report on one or more of Washington's agricultural products and/or natural resources. Make pictures to go along with your report.

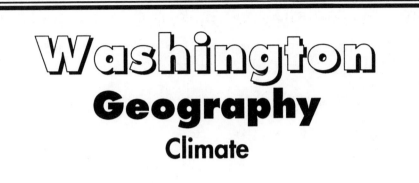

New Words to Learn:
Find the words in a dictionary and write the meanings on the line.

1. **annual:** _____

2. **Celsius:** _____

3. **Fahrenheit:** _____

4. **fiction** (fictitious)**:** _____

5. **precipitation:** _____

6. **sleet:** _____

Washington
Climate

Washington has a milder climate than any other state that is as far north. Westerly winds from the Pacific Ocean help keep summers cool and winters warm.

The state's lowest temperature ever recorded was –48°F (**Fahrenheit**). It occurred at Mazama and at Winthrop on December 30, 1968.

Make a map of the average low temperatures.

Complete this map...

Use this key. Color each of the temperature ranges the correct color. Make sure you color by the correct number. (Complete the compass rose.)

January
Average of Daily Low Temperatures

32° to 36° ① – yellow   16° to 24° ③ – orange

24° to 32° ② – red   8° to 16° ④ – green

0° to 8° ⑤ – blue

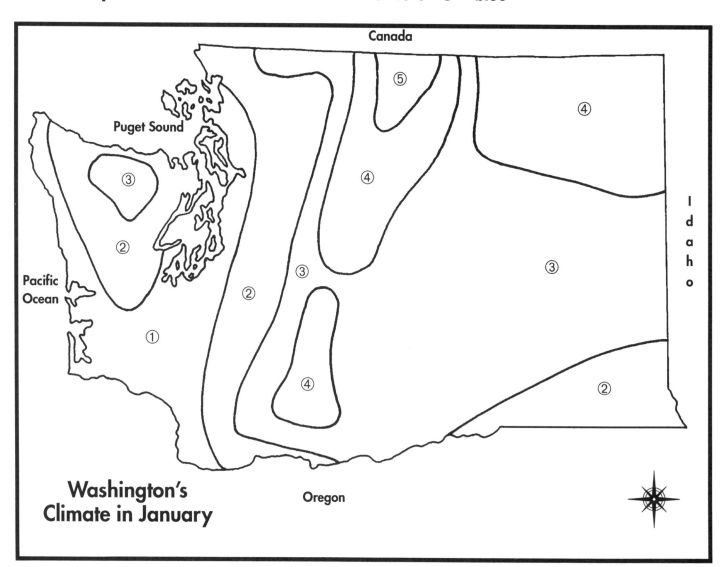

Washington's Climate in January

Washington
Climate

Washington's coast averages only about 5 inches of snowfall per year. However, Mount Rainier receives 50-75 inches on its lower slopes and over 500 inches on its higher slopes. The higher slopes are covered with snow throughout the year.

The heaviest snowfall ever recorded in the entire United States occurred in 1970-1971, at Paradise Ranger Station on Mount Rainier.

Make a map of the average high temperatures.

Complete this map...

Use this key. Color each of the temperature ranges the correct color. Make sure you color by the correct number. (Complete the compass rose.)

January
Average Daily
High Temperatures

44° to 52° ① – yellow   28° to 36° ③ – orange

36° to 44° ② – red   20° to 28° ④ – green

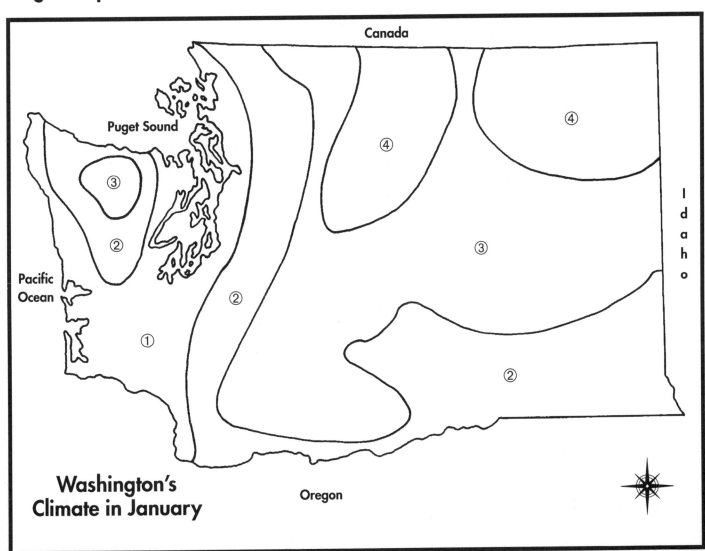

Washington's Climate in January

Washington
Climate

The moist winds from the Pacific Ocean bring a lot of rain to the western part of the state. However, by the time the winds and clouds cross the Cascade Mountains and reach eastern Washington, they have lost much of their moisture. As a result, the eastern portion of the state has a drier climate than the western part. Much of the eastern area is semi-desert, with very hot summer temperatures.

Make a map of the average low temperatures.

Complete this map...

Use this key. Color each of the temperature ranges the correct color. Make sure you color by the correct number. (Complete the compass rose.)

July
Average Daily Low Temperatures

56° to 64° ① – yellow   48° to 56° ② – orange

40° to 48° ③ – red

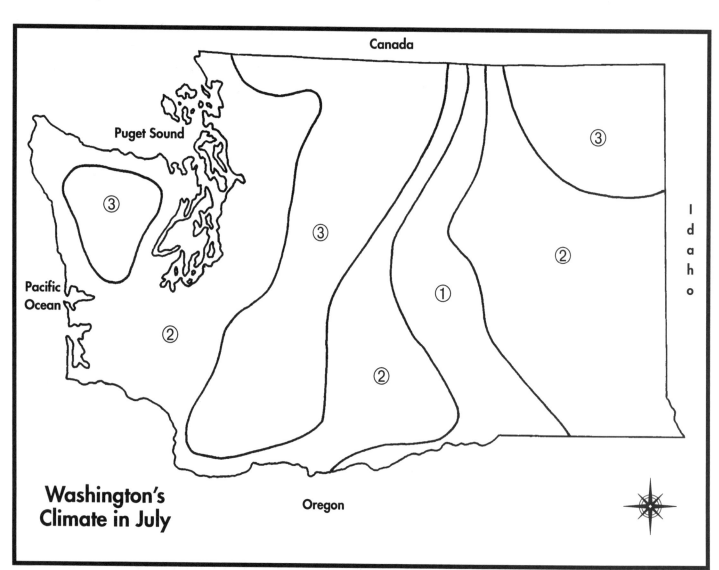

Canada

Puget Sound

③

Pacific Ocean

③

②

③

②

②

①

②

③

Idaho

Washington's Climate in July

Oregon

Washington
Climate

Name _____

Date _____

The highest temperature ever recorded in Washington was 118°F., on July 24, 1928. It was recorded near Wahluke. On August 5, 1961, Ice Harbor Dam in the southeastern part of the state also recorded a temperature of 118°F.

Make a map of the average high temperatures.

Complete this map...

Use this key. Color each of the temperature ranges the correct color. Make sure you color by the correct number. (Complete the compass rose.)

88° to 96° ① – yellow   72° to 80° ③ – orange

80° to 88° ② – red   64° to 72° ④ – green

July
Average Daily
High Temperatures

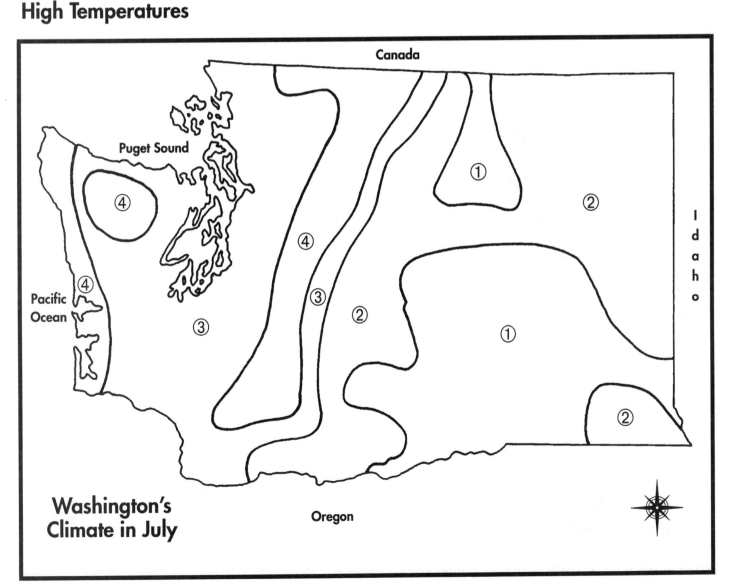

Washington's Climate in July

Name _____

Date _____

Another interesting type of map you can make is one that shows the average **annual** rainfall. (**Precipitation** includes the amount of rainfall, melted snow, **sleet** and other forms of moisture which fall from the sky.)

Precipitation in parts of the Olympic Peninsula averages over 135 inches per year. Washington's Central Plateau only receives 6 inches per year.

Make a map of the average precipitation.

Complete this map...

Use this key. Color each of the precipitation ranges the correct color. Make sure you color by the correct number. (Complete the compass rose.)

95" to 150" ① – yellow   48" to 95" ② – orange

24" to 48" ③ – red   12" to 24" ④ – green   0" to 12" ⑤ – blue

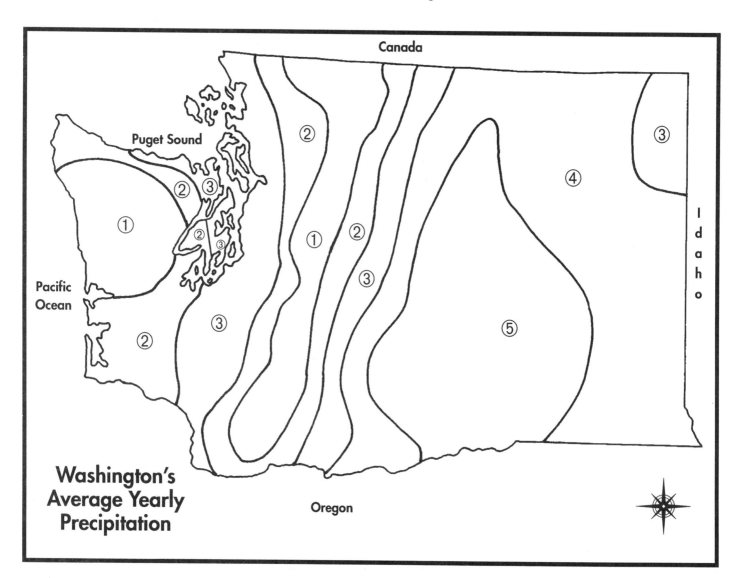

Washington's Average Yearly Precipitation

Washington
Climate

Name _____

Date _____

REVIEW QUESTIONS

Write the correct answer to complete the sentences.

1. The _____ winds from the _____ _____ bring a lot of _____ to the _____ part of Washington.

2. The _____ _____ averages 135 inches of precipitation per year.

3. The heaviest _____ in U.S. history occurred at _____ .

4. The _____ _____ only gets 6 inches of _____ per year.

5. The eastern part of the state has a _____ climate than the _____ part. Much of the eastern part is _____

6. The _____ _____ ever recorded in Washington was 118°F., on _____ . _____ also recorded the same temperature _____ years later.

7. Precipitation includes the amount of _____ , _____ and _____ .

Write the correct answer in the space provided. (You may need to use a map.)

8. What is January's average daily high temperature in the northeast corner of the state? _____

9. What is January's average daily low temperature in the southeast corner of the state? _____

10. What is July's average daily high temperature along the Pacific coastline?

_____

11. What is July's average daily low temperature in the southeastern and much of the western part of Washington? _____

12. What is Washington's average yearly precipitation along the Puget Sound?

_____

13. Explain why Washington has a milder climate than other states as far north.

_____

☆☆ **Bonus Activity**

Write a true or **fictitious** story about an adventure you or somebody else had in freezing winter or blistering hot summer. Be specific with the details.
Make pictures to go along with your adventure.

NOTES & Doodles

New Words to Learn:

Find the words in a dictionary and write the meanings on the line.

1. **border:**_____

2. **boundary:** _____

3. **city:** _____

4. **contiguous:**_____

5. **political:**_____

6. **state:** _____

Washington
Political Features

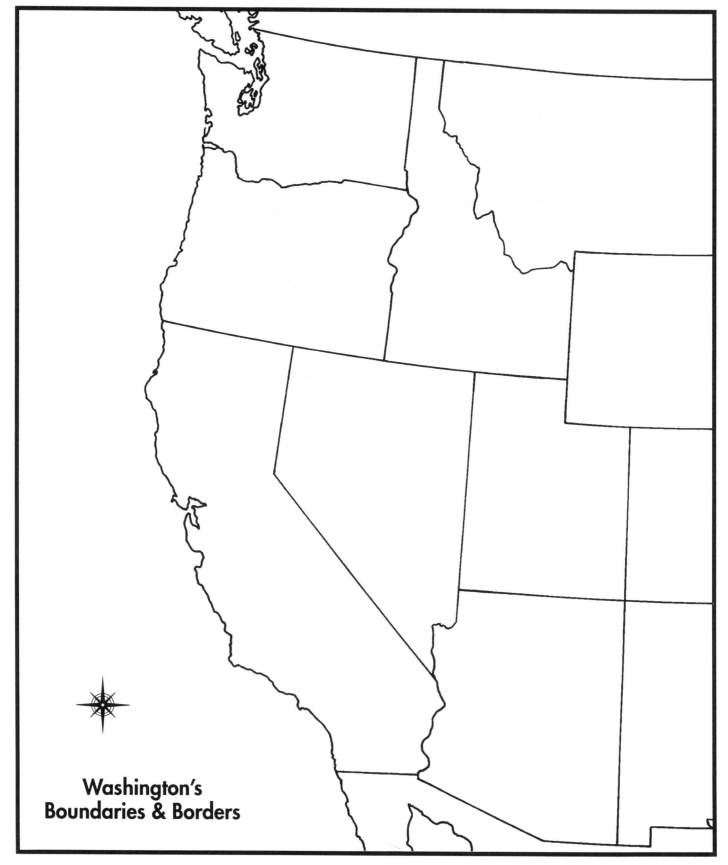

Washington's
Boundaries & Borders

Washington
Political Features

Name _____

Date _____

Boundaries & Borders

In order to understand the political features of Washington, it is important to see how most of the continents are generally divided up by governments.

From your definition of **political**, you learned it refers to a governmental organization. Keeping this in mind, here is the general development of governments, each existing within the larger one before it.

(Notice the words in **bold type**.)

1. Five of the seven **continents** have more than one **country** inside them. (Australia is only one country, and no government rules Antarctica.)

2. Countries usually have several smaller divisions within them. The United States calls these smaller divisions **states**. Canada calls these smaller divisions *provinces*.

3. Within each of our states there are several smaller governmental agencies called **counties**.

4. These counties usually have several **cities** within their boundaries.

All, or just one, of the above divisions could be drawn on a map. This type of map would be called a political **boundary** map. Political boundary maps are probably the most commonly used maps. They show the areas "ruled" by the different governments.

Do these things using the map provided.

Make sure you do these in order and exactly as the directions say.

1. Complete the compass rose.

2. Washington's nickname is *The Evergreen State*. Color it green.

3. Label Washington's bordering states and then color them yellow.

4. Label Canada. Color it a light brown or tan.

5. Color Mexico (the country south of the United States) purple or red.

6. Color the Pacific Ocean on Washington's west coast a light blue.

7. Write the names of any of the other states you know on the map.
   (You can also use another resource book or map to find the names of the rest of the states.)

8. Choose different colors to use on the rest of the states.

Washington
Political Features

Name _____

Date _____

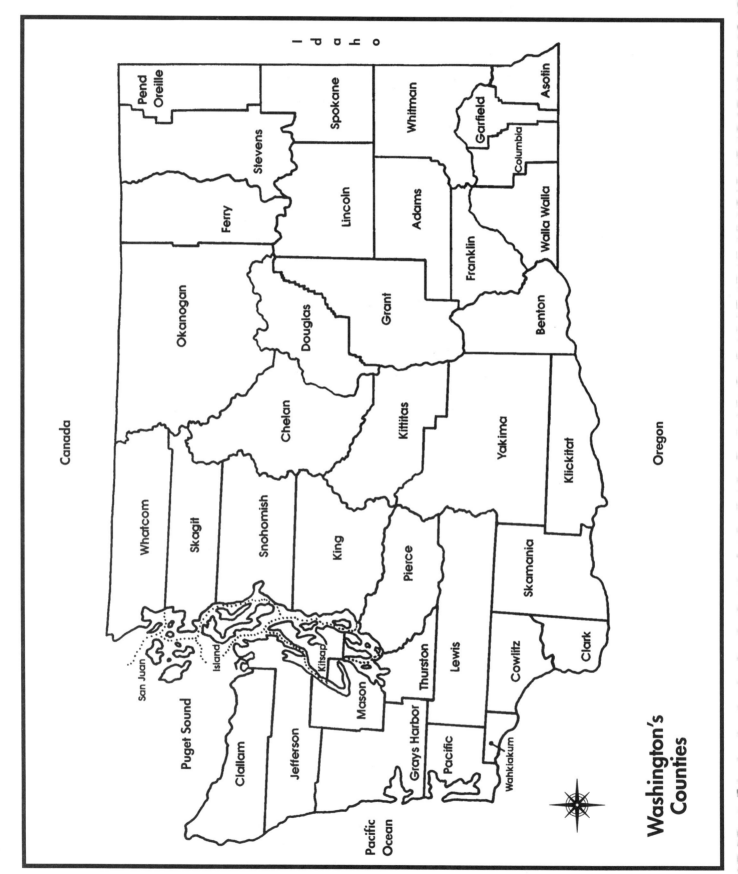

Washington's Counties

Washington
Political Features

Name _____

Date _____

Counties & Cities

The state of Washington has a total of 39 counties and hundreds of cities and towns. (Towns generally have fewer people living in them than cities.) A county usually has several cities within its boundaries. The county government and laws generally have more power than city governments.

Washington's *largest county* in area (size) is Okanogan. It is located in the north-central part of the state.

King County is Washington's *largest county* according to **population**. Seattle is located within King County, and is the largest *city*, according to population, in Washington. (Whenever somebody talks about the size of cities, they are almost always referring to the city's population.)

San Juan County is the smallest county in Washington according to size. Garfield is the least populated county.

Do these things using the map provided.

1. Write the name of the county where you live on the line.

_____

2. On the map provided, put a black dot in the county where you live. Write the name of your city or town (or closest city or town) next to the dot you just drew.

3. Color the county where you live your favorite color.

4. If you do not live in San Juan County, color it a light gray color.

5. If you do not live in King County, color it with light gray stripes.

6. If you do not live in Okanogan County, put gray dots in it.

7. Color the Pacific Ocean dark blue.

8. Color Puget Sound light blue.

9. Color the rest of Washington one of your favorite colors not yet used.

☆☆ **Bonus Activity**

Using the counties map provided and other paper, write the names of the counties in alphabetical order. Using another resource book, make a list of the counties in order of population (largest to smallest) and/or land area (largest to smallest).

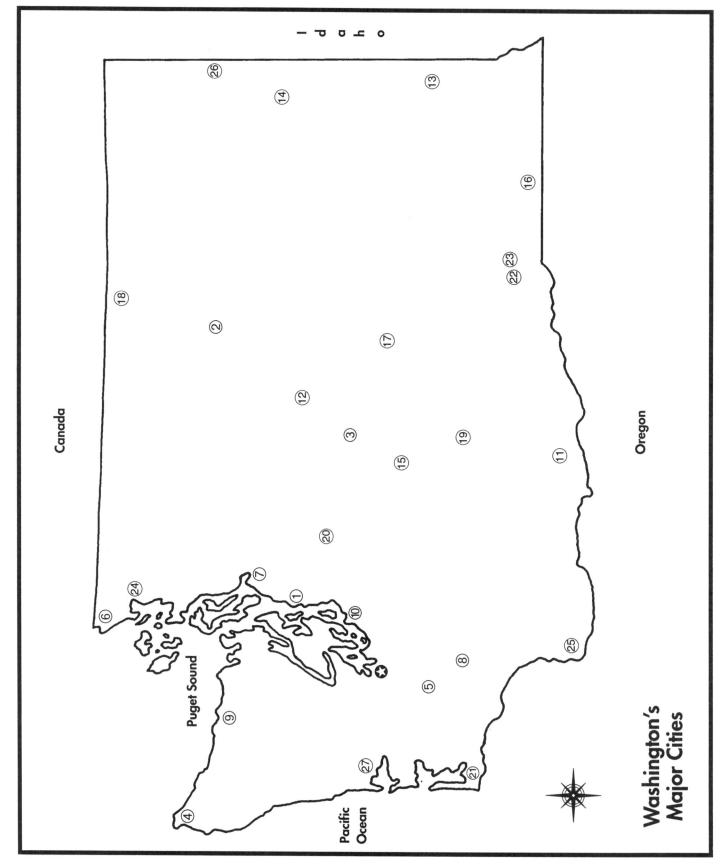

Idaho

Canada

Oregon

26

14

13

16

23
22

18

2

17

12

3

19

15

11

20

7

24

1

6

10

Puget Sound

8

5

9

25

27

21

4

Pacific Ocean

Washington's Major Cities

Washington
Political Features

Name _____

Date _____

Keys, Type Styles & Symbols

It can sometimes get confusing when you are trying to read maps. However, there are some things that help make it easier and less confusing.

Most maps provide a key that will help you know what certain symbols mean. (You have used keys for coloring the maps in the *Economic Features* section of this book.) The key also shows you that the words typed or colored differently mean different things. For example:

1. Names of states will usually be printed in **BLACK, TALL, ALL–CAPITAL LETTERS**.

2. Names of counties will be printed in smaller, ALL–CAPITAL LETTERS. They are usually printed in red or another color.

3. Names of small cities and towns are usually printed in black, with a light type. Only the first letter of each city is capitalized. A small, black dot (•) almost always shows the location of cities or towns.

4. The larger cities are printed the same as the smaller ones, **but they are printed in larger and bolder type**.

5. The location of the state's capital city usually has a circle with a star (similar to one like this ✪) inside it, instead of a small black dot.

Map keys can tell you many others things about maps, such as where airports are located, the size of roads, or just about anything else.

Do these things using the map provided.

1. Write the names of the bordering states, Canada, Puget Sound and the Pacific Ocean in the correct places.

2. Write the names of the cities by the correct number or symbol. Make sure you print them *exactly* the way they are printed here.

3. (You guessed it!) The last thing to do — complete the compass rose.

SEATTLE ①	**EVERETT** ⑦	**SPOKANE** ⑭	Long Beach ㉑
Omak ②	Mossyrock ⑧	**ELLENSBURG** ⑮	**KENNEWICK** ㉒
WENATCHEE ③	**PORT ANGELES** ⑨	**WALLA WALLA** ⑯	**PASCO** ㉓
OLYMPIA ✪	**TACOMA** ⑩	**MOSES LAKE** ⑰	**BELLINGHAM** ㉔
Neah Bay ④	**GOLDENDALE** ⑪	Oroville ⑱	**VANCOUVER** ㉕
Centralia ⑤	Chelan ⑫	**YAKIMA** ⑲	Newport ㉖
Blaine ⑥	**PULLMAN** ⑬	Snoqualmie ⑳	**ABERDEEN** ㉗

Washington
Political Features

REVIEW QUESTIONS

Circle the best answer to each question.

1. What state borders Washington on the south?
   a. Idaho   b. Oregon   c. Arizona   d. California

2. What is the largest county (in population) in Washington?
   a. Pierce   b. Spokane   c. King   d. Garfield

3. How many continents are governed by one country?
   a. one   b. two   c. five   d. seven

4. Where do you find out what a symbol on a map means?
   a. globe   b. dots   c. key   d. top

5. What state borders Washington on the east?
   a. Idaho   b. Oregon   c. Arizona   d. California

6. How many continents are governed by more than one country?
   a. one   b. two   c. five   d. seven

7. What Washington city is largest in population?
   a. Canada   b. Olympia   c. Tacoma   d. Seattle

8. What is the capital city of Washington?
   a. Spokane   b. Olympia   c. Tacoma   d. Seattle

9. How many counties are in Washington?
   a. 40   b. 28   c. 38   d. 39

10. What country is to the north of Washington?
    a. Canada   b. Alaska   c. Mexico   d. Oregon

Write the correct answer in the space provided.

11. List the following governmental organizations in order of size and authority. List them largest to smallest (left to right). **city   state   county   country**

1. _____   2. _____   3. _____   4. _____

☆☆ Bonus Activity
Using another resource book, write a report about any city or county located in Washington, or any state or country mentioned in this section. Find or make pictures to go with it.

Section Seven

Washington Geography
Review Activities

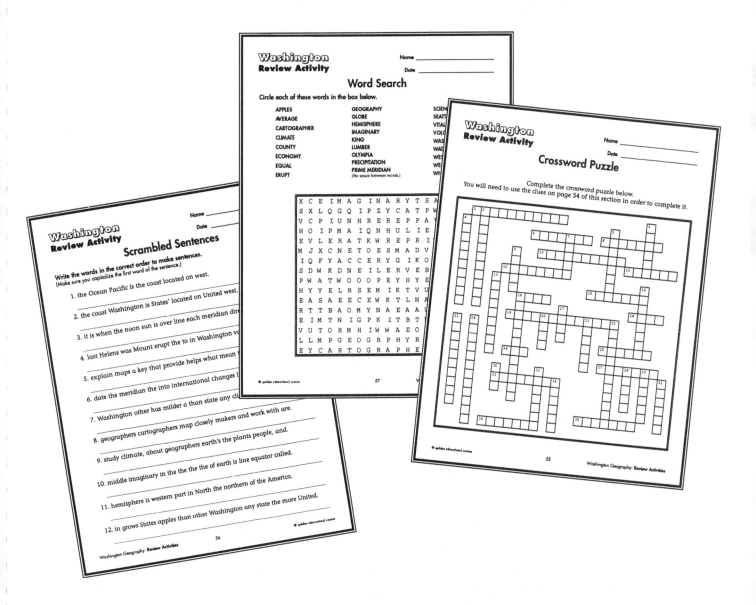

Name _____

Date _____

Crossword Puzzle

Across

1. This accounts for about 19% of Washington's total economy.
6. The management (earning and spending) of a state's money.
8. The governmental structure that has states, counties and cities under its authority.
10. This large bay in Washington was named after Captain Vancouver's lieutenant.
11. This continent is actually a peninsula of Asia.
12. Mount Rainier is the highest _____ in Washington state.
15. The capital city of Washington.
16. There are usually several of these within each county.
18. Washington's most populated county.
19. This longitude line runs through Greenwich, England, and is numbered zero degrees.
25. There are fifty of these that make up the United States of America.
26. The summer climate in the eastern part of Washington.
27. Movement from side-to-side.
33. Name the last Washington volcano to erupt.
35. This imaginary line separates the northern and southern hemispheres.
36. The mountain range separating eastern and western Washington.

Down

2. Scientists who study the earth and the life on it.
3. A _____ shows where one state begins and another ends.
4. The name of the state in the northwest corner of the *contiguous* United States.
5. A state's *border* is also known as its _____ .
7. There is one on the east coast and the west coast of the United States.
9. A spherical model of the earth, showing continents and seas.
13. *Prime* means _____ .
14. An imaginary line that measures a distance to the north or the south of the equator.
16. A person who makes maps.
17. Washington is in the _____ .
20. This direction is always on the right side of maps.
21. The distance measured from one latitude or longitude to the next.
22. The United States is on this continent.
23. Half of a ball-shaped figure.
24. Which continent is mostly in the southwestern hemisphere?
28. Geographers study many things about the _____ .
29. Every year; every twelve months.
30. The abbreviation of the *United States of America*.
31. Soil that is good for growing crops is called _____ soil.
32. San Juan is Washington's smallest _____ according to size.
34. Winter, spring, summer and fall (also called autumn) are each a _____ .

Crossword Puzzle

Complete the crossword puzzle below.
You will need to use the clues on page 54 of this section in order to complete it.

Washington
Review Activity

Name _____

Date _____

Scrambled Sentences

Write the words in the correct order to make sentences.
(Make sure you capitalize the first word of the sentence.)

1. the Ocean Pacific is the coast located on west.

_____

2. the coast Washington is States' located on United west.

_____

3. it is when the noon sun is over line each meridian directly.

_____

4. last Helens was Mount erupt the to in Washington volcano Saint.

_____

5. explain maps a key that provide helps what mean the symbols.

_____

6. date the meridian the into international changes line prime.

_____

7. Washington other has milder a than state any climate northern.

_____

8. geographers cartographers map closely makers and work with are.

_____

9. study climate, about geographers earth's the plants people, and.

_____

10. middle imaginary in the the the the of earth is line equator called.

_____

11. hemisphere is western part in North the northern of the America.

_____

12. in grows States apples than other Washington any state the more United.

_____

Name _____

Date _____

Word Search

Circle each of these words in the box below.

APPLES

AVERAGE

CARTOGRAPHER

CLIMATE

COUNTY

ECONOMY

EQUAL

ERUPT

GEOGRAPHY

GLOBE

HEMISPHERE

IMAGINARY

KING

LUMBER

OLYMPIA

PRECIPITATION

PRIME MERIDIAN
(No space between words.)

SCIENCE

SEATTLE

VITAL

VOLCANO

WASHINGTON

WATER

WEST

WESTERN

WHEAT

```
X C E I M A G I N A R Y T S A D
S X L Q G Q I P Z Y C A T P W A
V C P I U N H R E R E P P A V N
H O I P M A I Q N H U L I E A W
E V L E R A T K W R E P R I W A
M J X C N E T O E S M A D V E S
I Q F Y A C C E R Y G I K O S H
S D W K D N E I L E R V E B T I
P W A T W O O P E Y H Y E E N
H Y Y E L R S E M I K T V U R G
E A S A E E C E W K T L N A N T
R T T B A O M Y N A E A A U A O
E I M T N I G P K I T B T U O N
V U T O R M H I W W A E O I Q C
L L M P G E O G R P H Y R L O E
E Y C A R T O G R A P H E R G N
```

MORE
NOTES & Doodles

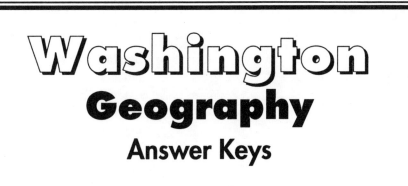

Suggestions for using these answer keys:

Answer keys have been provided for each of the sections in this book. We suggest that answer keys be made available to your students in order for them to correct their own work. If your students can use the answer keys provided in this section, duplicate and laminate them and allow students to check their own work (except for the answers that need to be checked by a teacher).

If your students are unable to use the answer sheets provided, duplicate each of the review questions and review activities. Complete them with a colored pen that is easily distinguished from the questions — red, orange or green work well. We also suggest that you laminate these pages and place them in a 3-ring binder to keep them organized and clean. This will allow them to last much longer.

World Overview – page 14

1. b. study of the earth
2. c. sphere
3. a. globe
4. southern hemisphere
5. imaginary; earth
6. Cartographers
7. prime meridian; earth; western

prime – beginning
north – top
hemi – half
south – bottom
east – right
west – left
sphere – ball-shaped
equator – middle line
meridian – "middle of the day"

Only 6 Needed: animals; climate; people;
plant life; earth's surface; earth's changes; oceans

Locating Washington – page 23 (page 1 of 2)

1. Africa, Antarctica, Asia, Australia, Europe
   North America, South America
2. North America, South America
3. Africa, Asia, Australia, Europe
4. Antarctica, Australia, South America

Locating Washington – page 24 (page 2 of 2)

1. north & south (up & down or top to bottom)
2. side-to-side
3. equator
4. prime meridian
5. Pacific Ocean
6. Canada
7. Mexico
8. east
9. northwest
10. north
11. west
12. northwest
13. southwest
14. 10° wide (approximately)
15. 10° high (approximately)
16. northwest
17. northern hemisphere; eastern hemisphere

Physical Features – page 30

1. *Teacher Check*
2. *Teacher Check*
3. *Teacher Check*
4. *Teacher Check*
5. *Teacher Check*
6. *Teacher Check*
7. *Teacher Check*

Economic Features – page 36

1. wheat
2. asparagus; barley; dry beans; dry peas;
   green peas; hops; potatoes; wheat
3. apples; apricots; blueberries; cherries;
   cranberries; grapes; pears; plums;
   prunes; raspberries; strawberries
4. water; timber forests; fertile soil (any order)
5. *Teacher Check*
6. Western Washington
7. *Teacher Check*

Climate – page 43

1. moist; Pacific Ocean; rain; western
2. Olympic Peninsula
3. snowfall; Paradise Ranger Station (Mt. Rainier)
4. Central Plateau; precipitation
5. drier; western; semi-desert
6. highest temperature; July 24, 1928;
   Ice Harbor Dam; 33
7. snow ; rain; other forms of moisture (any order)
8. 20° to 28°
9. 24° to 32°
10. 64° to 72°
11. 48° to 56°
12. 24 inches to 48 inches
13. Westerly winds from the Pacific Ocean keep
    summers cool and winters warm.

Political Features – page 52

1. b. Oregon
2. c. King
3. a. one
4. c. key
5. a. Idaho
6. c. five
7. d. Seattle
8. b. Olympia
9. d. 39
10. a. Canada
11. country; state;
    county; city

Washington
Geography

Review Activities – page 55
Crossword Puzzle
(Top Left)

Review Activities – page 56
Scrambled Sentence
(Lower Left)

Review Activities – page 57
Word Search
(Lower Right)

Scrambled Sentences – page 56

1. The Pacific Ocean is located on the west coast.
2. Washington is located on the United States' west coast.
3. It is noon when the sun is directly over each meridian line.
4. Mount Saint Helens was the last volcano to erupt in Washington.
5. Maps provide a key that helps explain what the symbols mean.
6. The prime meridian changes into the international date line.
7. Washington has a milder climate than any other northern state.
8. Cartographers are map makers and work closely with geographers.
9. Geographers study about the earth's climate, people, and plants.
10 The imaginary line in the middle of the earth is called the equator.
11. North America is in the northern part of the western hemisphere.
12. Washington grows more apples than any other state in the United States.

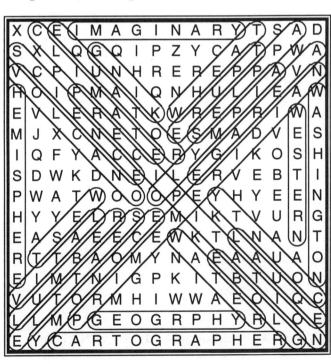

CREATING LINE DESIGNS

Students use a straight edge to sequentially connect dots in order to create geometric designs. These activities develop visual perception and eye-hand coordination as they build students' self-confidence. Each book has twenty activities and completed designs, which can be used for the answer key. *Teacher instructions are included.*

BOOK 1 #1001 . . . . K-1st
BOOK 2 #1002 . . . . 1st-3rd
BOOK 3 #1003 . . . . 3rd-5th
BOOK 4 #1004 . . . . 4th-7th

DESIGNS IN MATH

Students create geometric designs by connecting the dots between math problems and the correct answers. These activities reinforce basic math fact memorization, following directions and principles of design. Each book contains 20 activity pages with one design per page. There is also a completed design that can be used for a correction key or made into a transparency for classroom instruction. *Teacher instructions are included.*

ADDITION #1006 . . . . 3rd-5th
SUBTRACTION #1007 . . . . 3rd-5th
MULTIPLICATION #1008 . . . . . . 4th-6th
DIVISION #1009 . . . . 4th-7th
FRACTIONS #1010 . . . . 5th-9th
FRAC.-DEC. EQUIVALENTS #1011 5th-9th

❖ ❖ ❖

BEGINNING MATH ART

Similar to *Designs in Math,* these books show students the fundamentals of design while they practice solving their math problems and then connect the correct dots with a straight edge. There is a maximum of 12 problems per design. Young students will enjoy completing the 20 activity pages in each of these books. *Teacher instructions and answer keys are included.*

ADD & SUBTRACT 0-10 #1013
K-1st
ADD & SUBTRACT 11-20 #1014
1st-2nd
MULTIPLY & DIVIDE 0-12 #1015
2nd-3rd

READ⬩N⬩DRAW
FOLLOWING DIRECTIONS

These workbooks teach children to follow directions through exciting reading and measuring activities. Students build reading comprehension, as well as measuring skills, by reading directions, plotting and then connecting points with a ruler to create interesting designs. Twenty activities in each book. *Teacher instructions, students' glossary of new terms & keys are included.*

BOOK 1 #1021 . . . . 3rd-5th
BOOK 2 #1022 . . . . 4th-8th

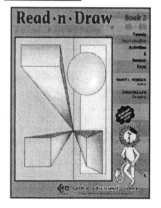

❖ ❖ ❖

USING A VISUAL GRID FOR SOLVING
MATH WORD PROBLEMS

Paring down to the most essential information, young students can now see and even understand the most essential elements/terms of a word problem. There are 35 lessons in each of these books. *Teacher instructions and answer keys are included.*

ADD & SUBTRACT 0-99 #1112
(no borrowing/carrying)   K-2nd
ADD & SUBTRACT TO 122 #1113
(with borrowing/carrying)   1st-3rd

❖ ❖ ❖ ❖ ❖ ❖ ❖ ❖ ❖ ❖ ❖ ❖ ❖

Other books available from Golden Educational Center. All of these books have an easy-to-read & use format.
Contact your local retail outlet or Golden Educational Center.

N. AMERICA COUNTRY STUDIES #1965 . . . 4th & Above
S. AMERICA COUNTRY STUDIES #1975 . . . . 4th & Above
FAR EAST COUNTRY STUDIES #1935 . . . . . 4th & Above
MID-EAST COUNTRY STUDIES #1936 . . . . . 4th & Above
CANADA PROVINCE STUDIES #1985 . . . . . . 4th & Above
CALIF. EARLY HISTORY #2911 . . . . 4th & Above
CALIF. GEOGRAPHY #2912 . . . . 4th & Above
WASH. STATE GEOGRAPHY #2106 . . . . . . 4th & Above

U.S. OUTLINE MAPS & STUDIES #1992 . . . 4th & Above
U.S. GEOGRAPHY #1993 . . . . 4th & Above
NEW **COMPLETE U.S. STATE STUDIES** #1995 . . . 4th & Above
CONTINENT MAPS & STUDIES #1905 . . . . . 4th & Above
LEARNING THE CONTINENTS #1906 . . . . . . 4th & Above
ECOLOGY ACTIVITIES #1205 . . . . K-3rd
ECOLOGY MATH #1105 . . . . 5th-8th
CREATING CALENDARS #1201 . . . . Pre K-3rd
HOLIDAY GREETING CARDS #1202 . . . . K-3rd